MOVING FORWARD:
WALKING IN FAITH NOT FEAR

To Mary,

Thank you for helping me!

With Love,

Monique V. Hines

Written by Monique V. Hines

Foreward written by Calvin L. Riley

(202) 870-8903

RSG Publishing LLC
www.rsgpublishing.com

Printed in the United States of America
Copyright © Monique Hines, 2017.

ISBN -13: 978-0-9825735-2-5
ISBN -10: 0-9825735-2-9

Library of Congress Control Number: 2017942393

Published by RSG Publishing, LLC
P.O. Box 116
Accokeek MD 20607
www.rsgpublishing.com

Author's Contact:
www.right-wayliving.com
Email: monique@right-wayliving.com

Cover design and inside layout by EYES INC. www.eyesinc.org

Page intentionally left blank.

Page intentionally left blank.

Disclaimer

This book presents views that are strictly that of the author. The ideas, opinions, and experiences of the author and do not necessarily reflect the views of the publisher, and the publisher herein disclaims any responsibility for them. This publication does not claim nor is qualified to offer in any professional capacity, advice concerning spiritual or religious counseling or any other form of consultation.

The author and publisher are not liable for any loss, health effect, or otherwise, any other consequences of applying any of the concepts or beliefs from this book.

Dedication

I dedicate my book to GOD the Father, the Son JESUS CHRIST, and the Holy Spirit living inside of me. Apart from Christ and the Holy Spirit, I can do nothing. *"For I can do everything through Christ, who gives me strength"* *(Philippians 4:13, NLT).* God is my mentor, counselor, provider, friend, healer, doctor, protector, companion, and confidant. God is my inspiration and motivating force moving me forward and most of the time pushing me into my destiny. Whenever you see me straying away from the cross, you always bring me back. Thank you Jesus for keeping me close to the cross.

I also dedicate my book to my father, Bennie Hines and my mother Anna V. Hines. I have always desired to make both of you very proud of me. Through the grace of God, this is coming true. To my father, I love you dearly. You are the hardest working individual I know, and you are a positive role model for my children. When God formed you before the beginning of creation, He did so having us in mind. God sanctioned you to be my earthly father, and my heavenly Father makes no mistakes. I am eternally thankful to God for allowing you to survive your heart attack many years ago. God could have called you home in 1999, but He knew we would need you now. Thank you daddy!

To my darling mother Anna, we have had our good times and some challenging times together, but you are definitely a great mom! I admire how you cherished your family, always wanting the best for us. You have dedicated your entire life to raising your children. Now I dedicate my story to you. Your inner strength is an inspiration to me. Going back to school with four children, a husband, and a full time career, you were determined to create a better life for us. Now you are a retired entrepreneur and a loving and doting "Mama" to my children. Thank you, Mommy, for always supporting me and standing by my side no matter what and providing for me and my children.

Thank you heavenly father for my precious parents. *"Honor your father and mother. This is the first commandment with a promise" (Ephesians 6:2, NLT).*

Table of Contents

Acknowledgements

This page is especially meaningful to me. It is important for me to publicly acknowledge these individuals. These "angels" have invested their time, money, and resources into me and **Right Way Living, LLC** in order for my dream to become a reality. I love each and every one of you! Thank you.

My children, Skyler, Dominic, Neko, and Mecca. You are my life! I am honored to be your mother. I love you! I am creating my legacy for you to carry on one day. You are the future leaders of the next generation.

Bennie and Anna V. Hines, my loving parents, thank you for never giving up on me. Even when I made it difficult for you to love me at times, you understand the true meaning of unconditional love. God bless you!

Uncle Ronnie, it is a blessing to have you in my life. Thank you for always listening and giving me godly advice. Your presence is like having another father.

Alicia T. Lopez, thank you for planting positive seeds in my spirit many years ago to start my own business. You pushed me forward.

Wayne (Thunder) and Penny Gamble-Williams, I have known the both of you all of my life. You have been such an inspiration. You are a good example of a husband and wife *team*. I admire the way both of you work together to serve our community. Penny would always say, "We have each other's back!"

Tiffany Marshall, my friend and spiritual sister. We met in high school as children, and now eighteen years later, I am proud to call you my sister. You are my personal hero. I am so eternally grateful that you saw "potential" in me. Thank you for introducing me to the Operation Hope program; it led me to Ms. Cynthia Harrison.

Ms. Cynthia Harrison, my mentor and friend. You are simply the best! I learned so much from you that I can now teach it to others. That is a good sign of a brilliant instructor. You are so dedicated to your students. When you told me that you would follow me throughout my career, I switched your title from mentor to friend. God bless you!

Jewell (Mama) Parker-Bailey, you are my spiritual counselor! Listening is a ministry all by itself. You have mastered your function. It is difficult to write about you in only a few sentences. You are the type of "Mama" every daughter should have. You inspired the first two words of the book, **Move Forward.** You are forever in my heart.

Geraldine (Gerri) Hopson, you are a prayer warrior. It is a pleasure to have met you in Bible school. Every time you pray for me, "**BIG**" things happen. Your prayers are on a hotline straight to Jesus!!! Thank you for your willingness to intercede continuously on behalf of others.

Sister Adrienne Cherry, you are a great encourager! We share a special bond as encouragers. I met you at my very first speaking engagement. I can never forget your spirit, so engaging and gentle. You are a kind woman.

Brother Calvin L. Riley, you are amazing! Every Tuesday night at 7:59pm I waited by the phone to hear your voice on the live conference call. Your wisdom has blessed me beyond my life's experiences. Thank you for mentoring me through my restoration process. "You do not lack power, you lack focus." You taught me how to focus with the power within me.

The world is waiting on your wisdom. Again, thank you to the entire Master Piece Mentors 360° family.

Sister Jeanette Riley, this book would not have been possible without your input. God always knows what to send you when you need it the most. He sent Brother Riley first, then you! God gave me a double portion of His blessings. Thank you for all of your wisdom and support.

I would like to personally thank the RSG Publishing team for all of its patience and dedication in publishing my book. This has been a pleasant experience. Thank you for excellent customer service!

Thank you to the rest of my family and friends for all of your loving kindness.

Message to the Reader

I am excited to share with you my wonderful new life. This is my story based on my spiritual journey. One year of reading the Holy Bible has forever changed the path and trajectory of my life! Before coming to Christ, I had never studied the Scriptures. After struggling for over a decade with anxiety issues and hitting a brick wall, I surrendered my will to God and allowed Him to take over. I would not be able to write my story if I had not repented of my sins and asked God to forgive me. I have been restored. Though I was not born blind, I was spiritually blinded by my sins. I used to be a dead woman walking. When life happened, I followed the world's example. Now, I follow the blueprint for right living outlined for me in the Bible and I am loving it! It took a divine encounter with the Holy Spirit to awaken me. I learned to have faith in God. I often feel like I am a part of a secret society, but, I am in the body of Christ; and there is nothing secret about us. Most people think of the word "church" as just a building. It extends beyond the four walls. According to the Scriptures, "WE" are the church. Jesus Christ is the head, and the believers make up the body of Christ. We are all here to work together for a divine purpose.

Have you wondered if there is something bigger than what your natural eyes can see? Is there someone or some being watching over you? Do you have questions that no human can answer? If you answered yes, then your quest has directed you to my story. This is not a coincidence. It was not by chance or luck or some sort of accident. You have chosen this book at the right time. Life is a journey.

"Enter through the narrow gate. For wide is the gate and broad is the road that leads to destruction, and many enter through it" (Matthew 7:13, NIV).

There are two realms: the supernatural and the natural. If I try to explain to you what happens in the supernatural realm, it will never make sense in the natural world. God's way of thinking is above our reasoning. Faith is believing in a guiding force that you cannot see. You have to believe it in your heart without a doubt. I have good news for you. My story is about purpose and salvation. I am one of God's messengers. Believe me when I say that God is real. Jesus Christ is the Lord and the Messiah.

Messiah: The expected King and deliverer of the Jewish nation.

Jesus was regarded by Christians as the Messiah of the Hebrew prophecies and the Savior of humankind.

He lives eternally and is seated at the right hand of God the Father. God is watching over us all. He is waiting on you to choose Jesus Christ, the risen Savior of mankind. This is a sign from God. There will be many signs to follow. I am an ordinary person called to do extraordinary things. *"Instead, speaking the truth in love, we will grow to become in every respect the mature body of him who is the head, that is, Christ" (Ephesians 4:15, NIV).*

I believe God wrapped His spirit in flesh and entered into the world through a woman named Mary as the vessel. Believing is placing hope inside an invisible realm. Blessed are those who believe and have not seen the Son of Man. God is concerned with my heart.

The only way to receive salvation is to believe in your heart that Jesus Christ died for our sins, and rose three days later. Before I wasn't sure if I was truly saved. Now I am positive of my salvation! Jesus came to save you and me. As you read my testimony of continual triumph over the enemy, my hope is that the Holy Spirit will minister to your heart for you to receive this message in love. God is love, and love conquers all!

"If you try to hang on to your life, you will lose it. But if you give up your life for my sake, you will save it. And what do you benefit if you gain the whole world but lose your own soul" (Matthew 16:25-26, NLT)?

We are given power through Jesus Christ in order to walk in Kingdom authority. I can see my way clearly. Some people never fulfill their destiny because they fail to realize their God-given purpose. If you have breath in your lungs, you have purpose. God is the only One who can give your assignment to you. I have my assignment on a piece of paper, and it travels everywhere with me. Even though I did not think I could handle the task, I wrote it down anyway. I have learned to motivate and encourage myself, even if no one else will. My steps are ordered by the Lord. Anyone I meet from this day forward has been sanctioned by the Holy Spirit. I will recover EVERYTHING that the enemy has stolen from me!

"The thief's purpose is to steal and kill and destroy. My purpose is to give them a rich and satisfying life" (John 10:10, NLT).

Are you seeking the Kingdom of God? He has the ability to satisfy your wants and needs. Have you taken the proper time to establish a relationship with Him first? Whatever your desires are, a better career, a spouse, or well-behaved children, God has the power to do it. Our spiritual houses should be in order. How strong is your foundation? God can restore the broken-hearted, give peace to the anxious, joy to those in pain, and healing to the sick. When you operate in God's grace, it will cause you to prosper in all areas of your life. You will have prosperity in your finances, careers, businesses, health, and relationships.

My surrender to God has become a daily routine. God wants me to accomplish something every day for the advancement of His Kingdom.

With God on my side who can be against me? The struggles I have had to overcome will bear witness to the trying of my faith. There is freedom that comes with hearing the Good News of the gospel. One day someone else will read my story and receive a breakthrough from generational strongholds and imprisonment of their own mindset. There has to be a point in each of our lives when we acknowledge that none of us can navigate through life alone. We need a Savior. God had to purge me of my ungodliness to prepare me for His use. I have been redeemed by God's saving grace. I wake up every day with purpose. Your purpose is based on things you can do naturally. Some people refer to it as talents; I prefer the word "functions." Think about what you enjoy doing that brings you absolute joy. When I help others, it empowers me to conquer my own circumstances. God has shown me so much that I must believe and continue to trust in Him.

"Seek the Kingdom of God above all else, and live righteously, and he will give you everything you need" (Matthew 6:33, NLT).

"If any of you wants to be my follower, you must turn from your selfish ways, take up your cross and follow me" (Matthew 16:24, NLT).

Testimonial

When I first met Monique V. Hines, I was impressed by her energy and her desire to serve the Lord. As she revealed some of her trials and pain, I noticed that she did not mask anything; she was very transparent in sharing her life story.

She loves her children: Skyler, Dominic, Neko, and Mecca. They are blessed to have her as their mother. She wants to leave a legacy for them.

Because of her faith, I know that she is well on her way to achieving her "possible" dream as a Empowerment Speaker, Minister, and a Writer.

I am truly excited for her as I watch her continue to blossom spiritually, all the while giving praise to The Father, The Son, and the Holy Spirit.

Jeanette M. Riley

Foreword

As I sit here at the kitchen counter doing some work on my computer, my wife is not far from me doing the same. She is taking time out to review a special book. Every now and then she speaks to me about some of the chapters, asks me a few questions, and has me look up words in the dictionary.

But when she stops her work and I stop mine, we spend some quiet time together, then I hear how the content of what she is reading is impacting her. I also see her being encouraged and inspired to continue forward in great things in her life. What a better feeling can a man get than to have his wife share with him some of the deeper thoughts in her mind and spirit that she has not shared before.

Thank you for bringing this project into my wife's life at this time. I know it will touch and inspire others inside and outside the body of Christ as it has both of us.

Calvin L. Riley

Page intentionally left blank.

MONIQUE V. HINES, AUTHOR

Introduction

"And they have defeated him by the blood of the Lamb and by their testimony, and they did not love their lives so much that they were afraid to die" (Revelation 12:11, NLT).

Over the last several years of my life, there have been testimonials of God's consistent deliverance of me from myself. Why me? It is not as if I am any more special than the next person. There is only one God and only one truth and He said that He is not a respecter of person, only faith. And it is upon this truth, found in Scriptures, that I have built my foundation. I have learned how to S.T.A.N.D. *(Situations, Testimonials, Authority, Nurturing, and Deliverance)*. God has been with me through every situation in my life.

Before, I could not see His hand in my life but now, I see Him everywhere.

It is said that there are two worlds – an earthly and spiritual. I was on a highway to hell. I had a first class ticket with a destination headed for destruction. For over ten years, I suffered in silence with anxiety issues. Spinning out of control, embarrassed and ashamed, I abused alcohol. It was 2008. I had an event to attend, and as usual, I had my own pre-party at home - I drank. I then attended the party and my drinks of choice were Hennessy, Heineken, and Patron. Despite their effect upon me, I would still drink. Crazy...right? Well, down went the Patron, then came the feeling of amnesia, there went my consciousness. Boy, was my perception and judgement lacking! It was idiocy to continue the same behavior and expect different results. Again, I abused the alcohol, and again, the enemy tried to kill me by convincing me to get behind the wheel. I did. It was dark and wet outside, and the roads were slippery. I was racing home, drunk. I had no idea that in a moment's time, my life would change forever.

Bum! It happened. My car crashed into another car on the opposite side of the road. I passed out! When I regained consciousness, it was as if I could taste the airbag that that had imploded in my face. Afraid and trembling, I dialed 911. It is still amazing that all I remember about the officer was that he was Caucasian. As an African American female, I was thinking this is not good. I can't forget the words he spoke to me repeatedly.

"Do you want to go to jail or go home?" The officer's voice still sounds in my ear.

I was instantly *sobered*. This Caucasian police officer had given this drunk African American female a choice. In the earthly realm, things like *race* matters. But when the Spirit of God is on the scene, all that superficial reality seems to dissipate, and it now one spirit interacting with another spirit.

"I can't go to jail. My mother would kill me!" My speech slurred.

The police officer took me home. He was an "**Angel**" sent to me by the Almighty God Himself. I looked at my car. It was totaled. I looked at the other driver and thank God that there was no serious injury. Somehow, I managed to walk away without a scratch. ***"God blocked it!"*** Grace had showed up, once more.

Chapter 1

Rise Up

"Daughter, he said to her, 'your faith has made you well. Go in peace" (Luke 8:48, NLT).

I am eternally thankful that for every trick and scheme of the enemy, God was already on the scene. In 2014, while I was seven months pregnant with my third child, I was diagnosed with pneumonia in both of my lungs. The Intensive Care Unit became my home for a while. No one knew my thoughts but God and me. Unable to speak with a tube down my throat, all I had was my inner voice, my inner spirit. I was terrified during that time. I just knew I was going to die. I had already placed one foot in the grave. I started thinking about to whom I was going to designate the care of my children after my death.　The Holy Spirit said not so fast. His power is phenomenal and mighty! One of my brothers, also a believer in Jesus Christ, came to see me. My brother began to read Scriptures to me. He explained how Jesus healed the sick. He spoke positivity over me.

He commanded me to rise from the grave; and into my spirit, came back life. What my brother did resonated with me, and I began to change my thought processes. The reality was within my womb was a seven month old fetus. Twenty nine years of age was too young for me to die! My story was not going to end like this. Besides, I had not done anything extraordinary with my life. What had I accomplished? What was my legacy going to be for my children to inherit?

I began to fight for my life and the life of my unborn child. I changed my thought processes and spoke only positive words and Scriptures. Hallelujah! Here I am! I am still standing on God's word and still fighting to fulfill my destiny! All honor, glory and praise belong to God Almighty for the great things that He has done for me.

After surviving this life-threatening illness, this is my account based on my journey. I had to move forward through all the anxiety, hurt, death, depression, defeat, doubt, fear, bondage, captivity, insecurities, rage, mental abuse, self-esteem issues, brokenness, and overall struggles of life. The biggest thing of all was to let go of FEAR itself.

Like Moses, I wandered aimlessly for years, but then God called me and redirected me. After my encounter with God, my spirit was awakened. Since then, a moment has not lapsed without me hearing or seeing God. I now view the world through my spiritual lens.

I was given access into heaven, when I was called by God. I never knew that God had a plan and purpose for my life. God knew me before the foundations of the earth were created. Before God created the earth, He gave me purpose. His love for me never ceased to amaze me. To have taken the time to personally fashion and design my life, in itself, tells me I am loved. His wonder and awesomeness still leave me speechless. Imagine the miracle of creation. Just imagine all that there is in the universe. Spectacular, isn't it?

In life, we have all experienced trials and tribulations. But, we must rise up like Christ rose. For a long time, I have allowed fear to govern my life and to cripple and hinder my walk with God. Now, I have replaced my fear with FAITH! I have learned to continue in life no matter what is happening to or around me. If I do not move forward, I will get stuck or, even worse, revert. I am continuing my walk with God by faith. Through prayer and fasting, I came up with my title for the book,

<u>Moving Forward: Walking in Faith Not Fear</u>. By allowing myself to be still, I was able to hear from God.

In the past, I had been so distracted by the things of this world that they drowned out the quiet still voice of the Holy Spirit. For us believers, our work and ministry have just begun. We have an "assignment" on our lives. God is for real and very much intentional. No one can enter into the kingdom of heaven without acknowledging God the Father, Jesus Christ the Son, and the Holy Spirit, who is our helper. God has a plan and purpose for each of our lives. *"For many are called but few are chosen" (Matthew 22:14, NLT).* We often ignore the call that God has placed on us. Everyone has an **"assignment"** for their lives. When you are walking, talking, operating, functioning, and utilizing spiritual gifts, you can and will fulfill your destiny. That is how we establish God's Kingdom here on earth. *"I knew you before I formed you in your mother's womb. Before you were born I set you apart and appointed you as my prophet to the nations" (Jeremiah 1:5, NLT).*

Chapter 2

Repentance

"Repent, then, and turn to God, so that your sins may be wiped out, that times of refreshing may come from the Lord" (Acts 3:19, NIV).

I started drinking at the age of fifteen. I stopped at thirty. I am still alive because of *"purpose."* I am grateful for another chance. The lifestyle that I was living was contrary to the word of God. I had to repent in order to receive God's grace which has been given to me through Jesus Christ. Without it, I would not have been successful. My change did not happen overnight, and it was not easy because it called for courage. We have to be willing to step outside of our comfort zone and make a commitment to excellence, not perfection.

We are taught to offer our bodies as a living sacrifice unto God, yet, I abused alcohol, smoked, fornicated, and used foul language – all displeasing to God. It kept me from knowing the true and living God. Though I am created in the likeness and image of God, fearfully and wonderfully made, special and uniquely designed, my self-worth or value in the eyes of God, escaped me. According to the Scriptures, I am guilty of many offenses. But, I thank God for His goodness, unfailing love, and willingness to forgive me. I used to look down on others because I was used to having everything given to me.

God called me one morning while I lay drunk in bed, and I heard it in my spirit. *"For the light makes everything visible. This is why it is said, 'Awake, O sleeper, rise up from the dead, and Christ will give you light'"* (Ephesians 5:14, NLT). We are to live holy and consecrated lives unto the Lord. I am called to be the light in a world full of darkness, and the light can never be extinguished. I am not saying that I have all the answers or that I have arrived now. None of us has it totally figured out. I am saying that life is a journey, and we are here to help each other and serve as an example for Christ, the best way we can. Even though at times, I do not intentionally sin, nevertheless, I am still a sinner. Every day I am extended new mercies through the grace of God. I surrender my will to Him on a daily basis.

Chapter 3

My Destiny

"Then the LORD said to me, Write my answer plainly on tablets, so that a runner can carry the correct message to others" (Habakkuk 2:2, NLT).

According to the Merriam-Webster Dictionary:

Destiny: A power that is believed to control what happens in the future.

Dream: A strongly desired goal or purpose.

Vision: A thought, concept, or object formed by the imagination.

For the last several years I have been going through a transition. Like a caterpillar changes into a butterfly in stages, my soul has transitioned in stages. I am a stronger individual with a sound mind focused on the love of God and His people. My mind is divinely orchestrated, and it is guiding me to perform a good work. God has a Kingdom objective, and it takes a strong person with a Kingdom mindset to help facilitate His masterplan. Each one of us has a Kingdom assignment. God created us as one body with many members. I am just a piece of the puzzle with some of the truth. It is not about me, but I thank God that I am included.

There is a ministry inside of all of us. We are just going to minister from different platforms. What are you passionate about? For which social causes do you have a burden? What laws do you have a burning desire to change? Have you given any serious thought to what your platform might be? Our purpose is deeper than what lies on the surface. God had to peel off many layers to get to the core of who I am. Up until two years ago, I had no idea what my role was in the body of Christ. The Holy Spirit did the necessary work, now I am being restored.

What is my purpose? It is working in the areas for which I am passionate. It is helping others overcome their fears. It is to set the captives free from the bondage of the imprisonment of their minds. I used to be a prisoner of my own mind. When I realized what my purpose was, I just ran with all of my ideas. But the enemy is always watching to see where he can set up a trick to try and take me out. There is liberty and freedom that come from hearing the Good News.

An awakening has taken place within me. Before, my soul was lost, but now I am found. I can see clearly now, and I refuse to go back to being blinded by the lusts of this world or my own desires. I am a new person created in the likeness of my Savior. Old habits have passed away. I am no longer attracted to the things of the past. God wants to establish a new thing through me and others.

I have discovered my platform. I am a empowerment speaker, emotional coach, minister, writer, and chef. The name of my company is Right Way Living, LLC. I am proud of my accomplishments because I stepped out on faith against all the odds. This is my ministry, and it is our company's mission to stand firmly on the Word of God. I am called to serve and lead a new generation of believers. There is a paradigm shift occurring in the spiritual atmosphere.

God is about order and decency; He is strategic and intentional. My first public speaking engagement oc-curred in 2015. I met a woman who was also one of the guest speakers, and instantly we connected. She is a part of an organization named Masterpiece Mentors 360°. God always knows who to send. The organization is a mentor-to mentor program. The outpouring of encouragement, along with the wisdom, has blessed me tremendously.

Abiding in the presence of the Lord has given me confidence. My validation does not come from people but from God. I know to whom I belong. Before I was born, God gave me these functions to perform. The life-style I was living prevented me from having a relation-ship with God. His spirit is Holy, and it cannot dwell in the midst of sin. There are seasons associated with my life. As a believer, every season is an opportunity for me to produce fruit. I was born for this moment to introduce my gift of writing. Every season is designed for me to succeed as I give my testimony to the world. People have real life problems, and they need real life solutions. There is hope for anyone struggling with addictions, spiritual warfare, poverty, despair, even a broken heart. God's love lifted me from my darkest hours of despair

My life is not in vain. There is a destiny I must fulfill. Even my finances have purpose. I do not spend money irresponsibly like I did in the past. The individuals with whom I communicate on a daily basis has to do with purpose. What I eat, read, and watch on TV or the inter-net all has to do with my purpose.

I have experienced a whirlwind of obstacles along the way. As a result of my time, relationships, and resources, I have been able to successfully outwit the enemy on all sides. People in society are being spiritually wounded and have no idea why or from where it is coming. It is a fight to recover what has been stolen from me. Without the mentorship, I would not have been able to finish writing my story. God created me to be a leader! *"This means that anyone who belongs to Christ has become a new person. The old life is gone; a new life has begun" (2 Corinthians 5:17, NLT)!*

Chapter 4

Eternally Grateful

"For I know the plans I have for you, says the LORD. They are plans for good and not for disaster, to give you a future and a hope" (Jeremiah 29:11, NLT).

In the beginning of my journey, I expected to write my book in three months. It has taken ten months to finish. Someone once told me, "Pursue great things, not greatness." I faced many obstacles along the way. Success is measured by our ability to continue on the pathway set out before you. Greater is He that is in me than he that is in the world. It took sheer determination. There were many sleepless nights.

I have successfully birthed my three **B's**: Business, Baby, and two Books, one of which is a workbook/journal. This all began with a pen, a sheet of paper, and a promise from the Lord. As I grew spiritually, my journal became my workbook. I have a mission to advance God's Kingdom.

Living a consecrated life unto the Lord is a wonderful experience. God makes me win! I am living my dreams. I mentioned to a childhood friend that I was in the process of completing my first novel, and she said, "You told me that when we were kids." I have no memory of the conversation. It blew my mind, but in a good way. Now, I understand why I had to endure all of my personal struggles. It was to give me a testimony. Deliverance is my testimony.

Life is a series of obstacles masked as difficulties. Life will pay me what I demand from it. Perhaps I did not go through as much as others, but my past experiences are enough for me. How much is enough for you? The road upon which I was traveling was going to lead me to a dead end. God was going to continue to allow me to be afflicted until I surrendered ALL. I cannot make it in life without the guidance of the Holy Spirit. Jesus bought me with a high price, His life.

I am forever grateful for the blood that was shed for the remission of my sins on Calvary over two thousand years ago. It is by that same blood I am able to live for eternity. Believing in Jesus Christ has sealed my soul. There is power in the name of Jesus Christ. In every situation I encounter I give God thanks because this is the will of God concerning MONIQUE VENETTA HINES. It is something about being gravely ill and then recovering that gives you an appreciation for life. All I have in life are the precious moments. I see the hope in my future.

My whole existence is my reason for being. I used to be afraid of dying but not anymore. My steps are ordered by the Lord. When my time is up, I am out of here. I just thank God that I am still alive. Time is just a block of space in eternity. My spirit will live on forever. I have eternal victory!

God is not concerned with rituals but rather my level of faith. It takes *faith* to make it in life. When my family and friends disappoint me, I have to rely on something greater than people. The only constant thing I need in my life, for the rest of my life, is my relationship with God. If I could make it on my own, then I wouldn't need faith.

God's ways are far beyond any human reasoning, and it will take me the rest of my life to fully understand who God truly is.

God has answered all of my prayers and has blessed me beyond my imagination. If He never does anything else for me, He has already done enough. I am a living miracle. I thank God for the birds in the sky, the trees, the plants, and for everything else that He created in the universe. I love looking at the clouds in the sky; they are a marvelous wonder to me.

Our faith has everything to do with our belief system. When I have conversations with people, I can tell when my dreams get too big for them because they try to bring me down to their reality. But there is nothing too hard for my God. He is rich in rubies, diamonds, gold, land, oil, and all other resources on the planet. I don't put limitations on what God can do for me and others. God is all that I need Him to be. NO matter how big or small the situation, I stay on the pathway to fulfilling my dreams. I don't look to the right or to the left. If I continue to move forward on the narrow path, at the end of my life I will receive a crown for a job well done. I have a mansion in eternal glory waiting for me. When I have accomplished my purpose, God will call me home. I focus on things eternally now instead of my present circumstances. He has the ability to bless me far beyond the natural into the supernatural. All I have to do is trust in Him to perform His great works! *"However, as it is written: What no eye has seen, what no ear has heard, and what no human mind has conceived the things God has prepared for those who love him"* (1 Corinthians 2:9, NIV).

Chapter 5

The Power To Choose

"But if serving the LORD seems undesirable to you, then choose for yourselves this day whom you will serve, whether the gods your ancestors served beyond the Euphrates, or the god of the Amorites, in whose land you are living. But as for me and my household, we will serve the LORD" (Joshua 24:15, NIV).

Over the past four years, I have been stuck in an impossible relationship. I was trying to do God's work for Him. It is impossible to fix any man. The work has to be done in his hearts. Only the Holy Spirit can do the necessary work.

Prior to meeting my ex-boyfriend I had never been in a "committed" relationship. I use the word very loosely because we were not joined together in a holy union before God. In the beginning, everything appeared to be fine. We began dating and seeing one another on a regular basis. He would call me frequently through-out the day but never after a certain time in the evening. The phone calls remained steady and consistent for over ninety days. Slowly, I fell in love with the time and attention that he gave me. We would often go out to dinner. But afterward, when I came home there was always this weird tension in the bottom of my stomach. The pain never persisted, so most of the time I dismissed it as a stomach ache.

Four months into our relationship I received a bombshell. I remember one Sunday afternoon very distinctly when he called as usual to check on me. Usually we would talk on the phone for hours, but this time the conversation only lasted minutes. In his haste to hang up the phone, the call actually stayed connected. Something in my spirit told me not to hang up the phone just yet. So I stayed on the call and listened for thirty minutes.

If there was ever any doubt in my mind about if he was being faithful to me, it was confirmed on that day. The man that I had been seeing for four months was in a relationship with another woman. She had just given birth to their second child, and they lived together. They even had a pet dog! I was mortified. It totally blind-sided me. I had never been intentionally deceived in such a manner. So many emotions ran across my mind that day. For the first time, I was heart-broken. I do not wish this kind of emotional distress on anyone. The next few months were very difficult for me to get through. Immediately, I broke up with him and stopped taking his phone calls.

Emotionally distraught, I started thinking about every moment I ever spent with or without him. I was in the relationship for several months without going to his house. I looked for inconsistencies in his story while trying to figure out how I missed the signs.

The only number I had was for his cell phone. Then the Lord started showing me big signs in his behavior. I could never reach him after nine o'clock at night. If I tried to call him, the phone would go straight to his voicemail. During the daytime, he would always call me first before I had the opportunity to call him. We were supposed to travel on a vacation together and we never went. There were promises he made to me, but he never fulfilled any of them. I would say the biggest sign of all was that his personality started to change drastically.

I spent a lot of time and energy trying to figure out how he was able to move so methodically and not be caught by either one of us. This explains the tension at the bottom of my stomach. Some women like to call it women's intuition. But there is no such thing. It is the Holy Spirit signaling me within my own spirit to alert me that something was not right about this situation, but I ignored the signal because I was blinded by lust. I had no personal relationship with God, but still God chose to reveal this to me. I am so blessed to have an awesome God!

I didn't have to hide in any bushes, hire a private investigator, or follow him around wearing a disguise. This news came to me divinely sent from the Almighty God Himself. I believe in my heart it was time for the lies and foolishness to be revealed to me. When God is for you, then who can be against you? God's plan will always prevail. I managed to obtain the other woman's cellular number, and I called her. She didn't answer the phone, so I left a message explaining who I was. I told her my name and the nature of the call to let her know that we were dating the same guy. The next day I waited anxiously by the phone for her to return my call. Ring…ring…ring…. It was an unknown incoming phone call. My heart began to race. I was driving, but I quickly answered the phone.

"Can I speak to Monique?" The voice from the other end uttered.

"This is she," I responded.

The caller said her name, then mentioned that she received my message and was returning the call. I asked her a few questions, and she told me that their relationship had ended years ago, but he was still living with her and sleeping on the couch. Now, the story would seem to check out perfectly. But how do you explain a newborn baby in the equation? It just didn't add up to me, and it sounded like nonsense, especially when he was then thrown out of the home they shared together.

Nonetheless, we kept in contact and eventually got back together, but things were never the same. In a selfish way, I felt good about the situation, like I won over her. Not realizing the obvious, that a dishonest person was using the both of us to fulfill his own selfish desires, I became very angry and vengeful towards him. For a long time I didn't want him to know that I smoked, but after I caught him cheating I didn't care anymore. Up until this point, I trusted everything that he ever told me. From the beginning it was all lies; he betrayed my trust in a major way. He even lied about his birth name and birth date. He was twenty years my senior! Who does that? You might do this if you're in the witness protection program. The amount of deception this man did was unreal.

Having two women thinking we were in a monogamous relationship with only him was simply evil. I had already given years to this man, and the more I thought about it, the more I became angry with him. So, I started planning how to make him pay for hurting me emotionally. For over two and a half years, I carried a grudge against him. My intention was to make him pay no matter what the costs. I began to cheat to make myself feel better. After I cheated on him, I couldn't handle being around him because of the guilt. I eventually told him what happened. He said it was like being shot with a bullet.

Two wrongs do not make a right; it only makes it worse, and it can become a potentially dangerous circumstance for all parties. Having my heart broken was one thing, but the heartache was unbearable. The longing for the individual and not having him around and the wondering who he was with or what they were doing were driving me crazy. Every day repeated thoughts of him being with other women would come into my mind. When this happened, it would kill me in my spirit to the point where I became emotionally bankrupted by my own thoughts and emotions. I learned how to hold my thoughts captive so that I wouldn't even allow the thought to become complete. *"We demolish arguments and pretension that sets itself up against the knowledge of God, and we take captive every thought to make it obedient to Christ" (2 Corinthians 10:5, NIV).* I stayed almost another year in the relationship before I became pregnant. I later found out that during my pregnancy, he resumed dating his ex-girlfriend again. This was incredibly disappointing to me. This time, I found pictures of them together in his phone and pictures of other women in his phone. I was heartbroken again.

He basically made it seem like there was nothing serious going on between them, so I forgave him again. I was in love with him, and I couldn't see clearly because my judgement was clouded by my own desires. I was tied to a spiritual stronghold in my relationship. Engaging in a sexual relationship with him created a soul tie between us. It was very difficult for me to break away from the spiritual bondage of sexual immorality.

I thought that Satan sent him into my life to make me miserable and destroy me. But I was wrong. Maybe God had used him to bring me to a point of surrender. All I know is that I was putting a man before my relationship with God. I idolized this person and made him my god. *"You shall have no other god before me" (Exodus 20:3, NIV).* My priorities were really messed up. I didn't value myself, and I had low self-esteem. Prior to meeting God, I had no direction in life. I knew nothing about His master plan nor that I was a part of it. Nothing in my life was going right for me because of the way I was living.

God is an original creator, and Satan can only copy what God creates. A boyfriend and girlfriend situation is a counterfeit situation to a real marriage. A boyfriend is a temporary fix to a permanent situation. God only intended for it to be marriage between a husband and wife. I was functioning in a dead relationship because I was outside the perfect will of God.

I will never again follow the direction of another man unless he is my husband and has submitted to Christ. God requires that husbands treat their wives as Christ treated the church. God loves me and wants the absolute best for me. The purpose of a man living a submitted life unto God is that it makes him account-able for his actions. If he knows God is watching him he will make better decisions concerning every aspect of his life. *"Wives, submit yourselves to your own husbands as you do to the Lord" (Ephesians 5:22, NIV).* I wasn't his wife. We were operating by our own strength, and we failed horribly. I was willfully sinning trying to please a man instead of pleasing God.

God knew what to do in order to get my attention. I fell in love with one man, and I had my heart broken three times by that same man. Now God has my atten-tion, and I know what my purpose is in life. Everything had to happen the way that it did to get me to this point. I count it all joy! God did not call me into a fairy tale. For a long time, I have waited for my prince charming to come to save me. He never came and will not come because he doesn't exist. I was looking for a savior and a way out of my situation. Jesus Christ is my Lord and Savior. My faith and hope are in Him alone. I have no regrets about my past relationship because it has made me a stronger individual. Now I have standards.

God made us all free will agents, and He gives us the option to choose for ourselves. In the past, I made some foolish decisions. My children are watching me now. I have an obligation to them to be a positive example of how a godly woman should live. The next time I will make better decisions. I will carefully choose who I date to be my potential husband. There is a saying "*a piece of man is better than no man.*" That is a lie from the pits of hell! No one should settle for anything less than God's best. I will continue to wait on God's promises to me. God created me for His glory. I will be sure to give Him all the glory out of my story.

Chapter 6

Accountability

"Children are a heritage from the LORD, offspring a reward from him" (Psalm 127:3, NIV).

I have been pregnant a total of seven times. After having three abortions I vowed never again to terminate a life God has given me. I can remember one of the experiences so vividly. A good friend went with me to the clinic. I was fine until I heard one of the nurses summoned me to another area.

"Ms. Hines."

In the back, patients were having their vital signs taken. This was some sort of prep room. I became overwhelmed by my emotions and ran into the bathroom, hyperventilating. I knew what I was about to do again was morally wrong. Knock... knock...

"Is everything alright? Do you need to speak with one of the counselors?" someone asked.

"No," I retorted and quickly wiped the tears from my eyes. If I had spoken to one of the professionals, she would have tried to change my mind. And I wasn't going to let that happen. I went through with it. After that, I would never forget the despair I felt. I vowed that it would be my last one and I promised God that I would never do it again.

My greatest challenge has also been my greatest joy in life; they are my children. It is not always easy to actually schedule time to sit down and write my story. Sometimes, I would type holding my infant. Until I became a parent, I had no idea the amount of time, sacrifice, patience, and dedication it takes to nurture a child. God has blessed me with four beautiful children. I have three boys and one daughter. My oldest son is named Skyler, my second oldest son is named Dominic, my youngest son is named Neko, and my only daughter is named Mecca. My first two sons are referred to as my purpose children, Neko is my faith baby, and Mecca is God's promise to me.

I am a single mom. Neko and Mecca share the same biological father. Skyler and Dominic's fathers are separate gentlemen. My oldest, twelve, is four years older than the second, who is six years older than the third, who is one year older than the Mecca. It wouldn't be appropriate for me to write about my struggles that I have overcome by the grace of God and not address being a parent. The truth is I am still learning "forward" how to be a better mother. The more I grow in my relationship with the Holy Spirit, the better my relationship has become with my children. It is a process, and it doesn't happen overnight.

Raising my children on my own is a lonely and difficult job to tackle. I had to move from the pain of my past into the pain of my future. So much of my spiritual freedom has come from letting go of the anger I felt toward the different fathers. I was upset because I felt deserted. Going to counseling helped me work through a lot of my anger. I needed to accept accountability for my own actions. It is easy to blame others for my decisions. I had to face some hard truths about myself. Taking responsibility for my choices instantly released me from spiritual bondage. No longer was I a victim of my circumstances. I went from being a victim to a victor! I had to move forward with my life. Now, I consider each of them my brothers in Christ.

My parenting skills before were so not commendable. I used to yell and curse at my children. God was not pleased with my parenting skills. As far as discipline was concerned, I spank my children. But there is a line that you can cross if you are not careful. Now, I stop and think before disciplining them. Is this how my Heavenly Father would react? Not every offense warrants a spanking. God is slow to anger. My children are on loan to me, and He has given me authority over them. I am a vessel used by God. My life has to mirror Christ, so that when they see me it should be a reflection of God's love. Their first example of a loving relationship begins at home. We are on this journey together. Through prayer, I have become more patient. He wants me to love my children into obedience. *"Don't fail to discipline your children. They won't die if you spank them"* *(Proverbs 23:13, NLT).*

In order for me to be a God fearing mother to my children, I have to remain in the Word of God. I cannot parent them according to the flesh. There are three voices: the voice of God, Satan, and Man. I had learned how to distinguish the difference among all three. Satan will try to use those who are the closest to us, including our children, for his purposes. When they are misbehaving, I rebuke the ungodly spirit inside of them in the name of Jesus. One afternoon my oldest son was playing on his game system, and I asked him to stop playing it for the day. He became very angry and started yelling and crying. I told him to go in my room for a time-out, and he started moaning and groaning in a strange tone of voice. He did not sound like his usual self. I immediately recognized that he had a spirit in him that was not of God. I began to pray over him, and moments later, he was back to acting like his normal self.

Every day at some point I experience mini storms. This is when the house is chaotic, both of my younger children are crying, the older ones are fighting, and I cannot even think rationally because of the noise level. When this occurs, I stop what I am doing and take a pause forward. I allow the negative energy to pass through the house, and eventually the babies will stop crying. Then, the older children will get along, and everything will go back to normal. Often I ask the Lord to help me in these moments so that I do not lose control of the situation. It never fails that the everyday challenges of life do not leave me worn because I have an expectation from God that he will see me through the storms with my children.

I am thankful for the four gifts that God has given me. They are my first ministry. I have an obligation under God to train my children up in the way they should go and witness to them about the Good News of the Gospel which is Jesus Christ, our risen Savior! We attend church regularly, and I read to them from the Holy Bible. My two year old can recognize the Bible, and he says words like Bible, praise the Lord, Amen, Hallelujah, and thank you Jesus! They are truly amazing.

Chapter 7

I Am Healed

"Holding her hand, he said to her, Talitha koum, which means little girl, get up" (Mark 5:41, NLT)!

I became very sick with double pneumonia. For six months, I had coughing spells at night; sometimes it would lead to vomiting. One weekend both of my sons came home coughing all night long. They both began running very high fevers. I took them to an after-hours urgent care facility. They were both diagnosed with the flu. That year none of us had been vaccinated for the flu. I chose not to be vaccinated because I was pregnant. I thought maybe it would cause more harm than good to my unborn child. I did not want to take the risk. After spending all weekend taking care of my sick children, I began to feel ill. I threw up at least twenty-two times within a twenty-four hour period. Nothing would stay in my system long enough for me to digest it, not even water. There was nothing left to vomit, which meant that I was probably dehydrated and needed some IV fluid.

I called my boyfriend with whom I did not live, to meet me at the hospital. When our call ended, I took a shower in case I was kept overnight. While showering, I became light-headed and almost fainted. This was a scary experience. I called him back, and he picked me up instead. On the way to the hospital, he asked me if I was having difficulty 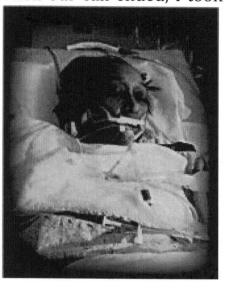 breathing, and I said no. It took a moment for me to actually process what he was saying, but when I thought about it, yes I was having breathing difficulties. We drove to the nearest hospital instead, even though it did not have a maternity unit. At this point, I was being treated for flu-like symptoms and was monitored for my breathing.

Finally, around 2:00 a.m., after waiting more than twelve hours, I was taken to another facility's emergency room. I began to feel better, and my breathing seemed to be regular again. I was joking and laughing with the EMT's. In the triage area, the ER nurse took my vital sign my blood pressure read 81/46. Everyone became silent. I was still running a fever, too. She took my vitals again; there was no improvement. The state of my health immediately placed me on the priority list in the ER unit. I was put in a room directly in front of the nurse's station, so I could be monitored by all of the nurses.

In my past experiences, going to the emergency room lasted for hours. Most of the time was spent waiting to be seen by the attending physician. This time, however, was different. I remembered the doctor coming in rather quickly. He informed me that I did have the flu and needed to be given a shot of medicine to stop the virus from reacting in my system. I hesitated with my response so he called my OBGYN's office. I spoke with one of the female physicians on call.

"Monique, I don't think you understand how sick you really are. The doctor wants to admit you into the Intensive Care Unit, so you need to take the medicine."

Tears began to stream down my cheek. I worked in the medical field for almost eight years as a nursing assistant, and I soon realized this was a cause for great concern. The doctor ordered for me to have medicine administered, and a few hours later I was transferred into the Intensive Care Unit. From the moment I arrived on the ICU unit, everything started going downhill as far as my health was concerned. My blood count was dangerously low. My breathing was out of control. Normal breaths per minute are generally between 12-20 beats for someone my age when the body is at rest. I was breathing 60 beats per minute. I also had to receive a blood transfusion. The doctors told my family that my body was going to tire itself out because it was working so hard to over-compensate. The baby was robbing me of all my oxygen supply. First, they tried to regulate my breathing with a CPAP machine used for patients with sleep apnea. Its purpose is to supply a constant and steady air pressure down my airway. It did not work. I could not get my breathing in sync with the machine. Time was running out for me. The doctors were very concerned because at the rate of which I was breathing, I could have gone into cardiac arrest. They explained to my loved ones that if that happened, they were going to perform a tracheotomy to open up my airway. A tracheotomy is an incision in the windpipe made to relieve an obstruction to breathing. This would have left me with a long road to recovery and a possibility of needing speech therapy.

The physicians made a decision to sedate me and put me on the ventilator machine.

The nurses would come in routinely and suction the mucus from my lungs. This process was very painful. They would push the tubing down until it reached my lungs, then pull the tubing back out very slowly. It felt like I was being stabbed in the chest with a razor blade. Every time it happened, I would end up in a coughing attack that lasted for what seemed to me an eternity. If someone put me flat on my back I would lose my breath. One of the nurses turned me on my back during one of the shifts, and I thought I was going to die. I would suction my mouth area to dry up the mucus that was causing me to drool constantly.

The baby was being monitored by the Labor and Delivery Unit several times a day. I received daily injections of heparin to stop my blood from clotting, and I wore a catheter. Therefore, being comfortable was the furthest thought from my mind. I changed my mindset from Monique, the former caregiver, to the patient. My mother and boyfriend never left my side. They would take turns staying with me at the hospital. I know it must have been heartbreaking for them to see me so sick.

My brother, an avid believer in Jesus Christ came to see me. He read Scriptures to me. He read them over me. He spoke life over me. He put God in remembrance of His word that Jesus healed the sick. He declared that I was healed in Jesus' name. He commanded me to rise from the grave; and my spirit heeded to the call. I made a decision to receive the Word of God over my life. I accepted it. I changed my thought processes. I was going to live as Christ intended. "I have come that they may have life, and have it to the full" (John 10:10, NIV).

My trial run lasted for roughly two hours. If this test was unsuccessful, then they would have had to do a tracheotomy anyway. This made my family very nervous. I brought my breathing under control since I had long convinced myself to be calm, so as not to have any panic attacks. My mental state was really being tested. Thirty minutes passed, one hour, then two hours.

After the two hour mark, the respiratory therapist came and removed me from the ventilator. Faith will move any mountain. Hallelujah! My God is awesome.

I could see the relief in the medical teams' eyes. It is difficult to put into words how I felt. The doctors told me afterwards how scared they were for me and how one of their previous patients had died in similar circumstances. Some of the nurses asked me how could I have han-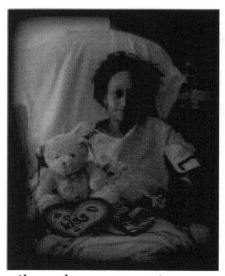dled being awake on the ventilator because patients on the machine were usually in a coma. I cannot remember what my response was at the time, but I know that it was by the grace of God that I made it. When I finally had a moment to myself, I was overcome by my emotions. I cried. God had taken me through this traumatic event to increase my faith so that I would begin to trust in Him. You see, Neko, the child in my womb at the time, is my faith baby.

Chapter 8

It's For Me

"Jesus asked, Will you never believe in me unless you see miraculous signs and wonders" (John 4:48, NLT)?

My mother purchased a Holy Bible as a present for me. She gave it to me on August 21st 2008. It wasn't enough for me to just have the Bible. I needed the accessories to go with it. I picked out a shiny pink Bible case to carry it in. It has taken me seven years to start reading the Bible. God began to reveal Himself to me through Scriptures. When I became serious about establishing my relationship with Him, He spoke to me.

In 2015, I took a course on how to study the Bible for yourself. This class was amazing. I grew in a matter of months with a zeal for the Lord. There are many different translations of the Holy Bible. I find the Life Application Study Bible to be an easier read. It is important for me to worship at a Bible teaching church. When I go, it is to hear a prophetic word from the Lord. I have a routine of doing spiritual assessments to evaluate my personal growth from my past experiences. The Holy Spirit does the checks and balances within me. If I do something contrary to the will of God, I am checked. A friend of the world is an enemy of God. It is marvelous to see Him working through me and others.

Because there is so much negativity in the world, I constantly try to surround myself with positive role models. I adopted inspirational and motivational strategies, combined with faith in God. The Word revitalizes my spirit. It is electrifying! He will always give the Word to me first on which to meditate. It is then I share it with others.

There are many tools I use to encourage myself and stay positive. One way is through preached sermons that I watch on the internet. I like to listen to sermons while I am driving to work, taking the children to school, being with my sister or my niece at home, or just in my spare time. It gives me another opportunity to connect with other ministries around the world. A lot of the time I feel as though the pastor is preaching directly to me. It is an amazing feeling, and sometimes I want to scream for joy at the wonderful revelation of God's word. I thank the Lord for the new mercies He extends to me each day. Wherever I go for the rest of my life, I will always look for the presence of the Lord.

I had the opportunity last year to sit in an open forum to discuss evacuation procedures in the event of a national disaster. One of my mentors invited me to give a brief testimony on my economic status. On the actual day of the event, I started feeling really nervous. The Lord brought back into my remembrance the scripture in *Joshua 1:9.* I began to feel overwhelmed by all the people in the room. So I excused myself, went to the bathroom and began to cry until my eyes turned bright red. Staring in the mirror, I recited the Scripture over and over again, and I began to calm down. I didn't want anyone thinking that I was unstable because I was actually very happy. That day I cried tears of joy because I was thankful to have an opportunity to share my story. *"Have I not commanded you? Be strong and courageous. Do not be afraid; do not be discouraged, for the LORD your God will be with you wherever you go" (Joshua 1:9, NIV).*

One of my best girlfriends today is a young woman with whom that I attended high school. We lost contact for a few years after graduating. In 2013, we connected again. But this time, our reunion was different. I felt the energy coming from her. She had a glow and a radiant beam. It was a divine appointment that brought us back together. God will always send you what you need. She has been such a huge blessing to me and my children. We are not only friends, but we are sisters, too. She told me about *Operation Hope,* a non-profit organization that teaches entrepreneurship. It was through the program that I met the program director who later became my mentor. With these two women, their testimonies, spirit, encouragement, advice, dedication, mentorship, and commitment to excellence has blessed me enormously. They are godly examples for me to follow. It is a blessing to see successful women who have overcome. I am grateful for both of them.

I met another *angel, an* entrepreneur who was being honored by the *Rainbow Push Coalition* for her community service last year. She hired me to cater an event. I prepared chicken and a mixed green salad. Numerous celebrities circulated through the room, and I met Rev. Jesse Jackson.

All I could do was think about the goodness of the Lord. It made my heart smile. It was never about the food. God wanted me to have this divine experience. His favor placed me before great people. Just think, a bucket of chicken got me into a room with one of history's legends. Everywhere I go now, I am looking for God to show up on the scene. I met a gospel poetry artist, and she signed the CD I purchased. Out of all the Scriptures she could have used, she wrote Jeremiah 29:11. It was a sign from the Lord. Another time while attending a workshop, one of the presenters walked over after the seminar and handed me a DVD movie. I had it for months before I watched it, and when I did the individuals were talking about finances and God.

When I am driving to take my children to school in the mornings, we always see inspirational bumper stickers and license plates referring to God. We have seen *2Blessed, Thankful, Trust God, Hope N Him, But God, 3 J1 and I've even seen trucks with words like "Keep Calm God is in Control," "Tree of Life."* Every time I see something motivational, it encourages my spirit.

I have noticed other things like street signs that say *Mission Drive, Church Road, Promise Land, Old Saints Road, and Enterprise Road.* One time I bought a pack of gum, and even the gum wrapper had something inspiring written on the wrapping papers. It is moments like those that truly warm my heart. Sometimes the messages come in the form of a person. I met a gentleman three years ago. He was a police officer on a motorcycle. I stopped him to ask a question, and we ended up talking on the side of the road in cool, fall-like weather for over three hours. The entire conversation was about God. It was a divine encounter and something I will never forget. Most of what he said has transpired in my life up until this point. One thing that he told me that I will always remember, *"Pray to God not to give me things that will take my love away from him."* I can tell you I have prayed that prayer more than once.

Another time, I was on my way to the bank while listening to a sermon by a female pastor. It was as though she was talking directly to me. She was talking about starting your own business and doing the research on the internet. One thing I distinctly remember was her speaking about airplanes and going to another level. I believed in my heart that the message was divinely sent to me by God. Ever since I heard the message, I have been seeing airplanes. One morning I dropped my children off at school and in the course of forty-five minutes, I saw over thirty planes flying in every direction. Every day I can see or hear airplanes and even he-licopters. I love it! It is a sign from the Almighty God himself to me! I feel so special.

Fortune cookies are another one of my absolute favorite ways to hear from the Lord. Before coming to Christ, fortune cookies never made any sense to me. Now, every time I eat a fortune cookie the verse written on the paper makes perfect sense. There was a hurricane storm that was scheduled to hit my state. The rain completely passed by this area. God foretold this meaning to me by way of a fortune cookie.

Lately, I noticed there are a lot of inspirational movies being produced. It has been a blessing to see the movies and view some of God's work depicted for everyone to see. Some of the movies left me in awe. I listen to a lot of *YouTube videos*. I thank God for using the internet to His advantage to showcase His children. There is so much talent in the world.

My niece, Alianna, is one of my biggest encouragers. She said this to me one day and I was so moved I had to write it down: *"Whenever God is talking, just listen to Him. Whenever you get mad, Just listen to your heart and God will tell you to calm down. God loves and cares about you so much. He always wants to take care of you and protect you from all the bad things in the world. He will always make sure you're safe with Him. God will never let Satan take the power away from Him. God will never let me do wrong in my heart. He will never, ever, let me choose something else that I love more than him. God will never choose someone over me. God will always, always, always be with me wherever I go."* At the time she was only five years old. There isn't a doubt in my mind; she hears directly from the Lord.

Chapter 9

Growth

"Work hard so you can present yourself to God and receive his approval. Be a good worker, one who does not need to be ashamed and who correctly explains the word of truth" (2 Timothy 2:15, NLT). According to the Merriam-Webster Dictionary:

Revelation: An act of revealing or communicating divine truth. Something that is revealed by God to humans.

Dedication: An act of rite to a divine being or to a sacred use. A devoting or setting aside for a particular purpose.

Wisdom: Knowledge that is gained by having many experiences in life. The natural ability to understand things that most other people cannot understand. Knowledge of what is proper or reasonable: good sense or judgement.

The beginning of wisdom is this: Get wisdom. Though it cost all you have, get understanding" (Proverbs 4:7, NIV).

"Study this Book of instruction continually. Meditate on it day and night so you will be sure to obey everything written in it. Only then will you prosper and succeed in all you do" (Joshua 1:8, NLT).

I decided to *rededicate* my life to Christ at the age of thirty. I have acknowledged before God that I was living a life of sin and destruction. Repenting of my sins was only the beginning--it was time for a real change to occur. I fully submitted myself to God. He gives me the ability to see spiritual truths through revelation of the text so that I can apply it to my everyday living. I used to be bipolar in my walk with God. As long as things were going well, everything was great. But the moment things seemed to go in another direction, I started to panic. This did not last long because the more I read, the more my faith level grew.

Patience keeps me walking with God. I used to be very impatient. If I waited too long at the grocery store, I would complain about it. God does not want me to go around grumbling and complaining. People should see God's Holy presence illuminating through me. God loves it when I praise Him in advance for the miracle before it manifests in the natural. Praise is my way, as a believer, to say thank you Lord for all you've done for me. It takes radical faith to believe in God to perform miracle after miracle. I believe that the same resurrecting power that raised Jesus Christ from the dead gives me life. I live my life with expectancy. Rejoicing is similar to praising, but I mostly rejoice after I have seen the blessings in the natural realm. God loves it when I rejoice. No matter how big or small the size of the blessing may seem to someone else, it is major to me. My situation could always be a different one. I would not switch places with anyone else in the world. No one can tell my story like I can. I live a blessed life above and beyond anything I could have ever dreamed for myself.

In 2011, I took care of a woman who was terminally ill with cancer. She never complained the entire year that I cared for her. The doctors gave her only months to live, and she lived for another seven years with brain cancer. Scientifically, she was a phenomenon, but, spiritually, she was a living miracle. She was a testament of God's grace: when anyone asked her how she was doing, this was her response, *"God is good all the time, and all the time God is good!"*

We bonded over the course of that year, and it impacted my life in a profound way. She always talked about the importance of a sound education and she encouraged me to go back to college. But that wasn't what stayed with me all of these years. It was her unconditional love for the Lord. Now I know how she felt because I am experiencing God's love from the inside out. She was a beautiful woman with a kind heart and gentle spirit. She was an angel sent to me.

God is everywhere. His Holy presence is living among us. I had the tendency to look up at the sky when I prayed. Now I just look all around me. I can feel God's Spirit on me, and sometimes it gives me a warm, tingling sensation on my skin. It makes me smile.

Sometimes I get frustrated, and I feel like quitting. That's when God reminds me to consider what Christ endured for me on the cross. Jesus was beaten, humiliated, and suffered for six hours a horrible and brutal death. So that one day when I have finished my course I can live forever in eternal glory with Christ. If Jesus can endure the cross and crucifixion, I can continue to run the race that is set before me.

It takes a lot of discipline to continue on the path of righteousness. There has been a trying and a testing of my faith but I have made a commitment to serving the Lord with a spirit of moral excellence. God has been too good to me, and He has shown me marvelous things. I am blessed to have God's favor upon my life. To whom much is given, much is required. I spend my time either reading, writing, or caring for my four young children. It is because of this regimented schedule that I was finally able to complete writing the two books. All of the honor, glory, and praise belongs to the great "I AM." I am nothing without Jesus Christ. He is the reason for every season and the only reason that I live.

Chapter 10

The Gifts

"And without faith it is impossible to please God, because anyone who comes to him must believe that he exists and that he rewards those who earnestly seek him" *(Hebrews 11:6, NIV).*

After I rededicated my life to Christ, I decided to become a minister. Being in the program was a wonderful blessing. I have met so many encouraging individuals from all walks of life. There are more good people in the world than bad. I also took an entrepreneurial twelve-week free training program as well as a biblical class at the same time. I kept feeling this urge in my spirit to read continuously in my biblical class. In one hand, I had my Bible, and in the other hand I had the manual for my business class. I was able to complete a business plan even though I never read any of the manual. I studied the word of God, and, as a result, the Lord gave me the ability to successfully complete both classes. To God be the glory! The training was phenomenal, but as far as the task of creating my business plan, I knew there was something divine at work. God was preparing me to write my Book. None of my experiences, past or present, will be wasted. My life has been uniquely pieced together before I was even born.

Another exciting event took place. God blessed me with the resources to pay off my previous vehicle. When I found out I was expecting my fourth child, I decided to get a larger vehicle to accommodate my growing family. My intentions were to use my tax return to purchase the car. I filed my taxes with the expectation of a few thousand dollars coming back to me. About a month later, I received a letter from the IRS explaining that my return had been intercepted by the federal government due to a student loan debt. That night, I cried. The next day, I stopped crying. Today my loan is no longer in default because I am making my payments on time. *"And we know that in all things God works for the good of those who love him, who have been called according to his purpose" (Romans 8:28, NIV).*

One afternoon after I picked my children up from school, I decided to stop by the Honda dealership. I asked to speak with the salesman that I had been corresponding with for months over the telephone. That day, I test drove the car that I liked; it was fully loaded! My children were excited. Naturally, we fell in love with it. I told the salesman that I needed to think about whether or not I was going to purchase it. Although it was a nice luxury car, it was clearly out of my budget. Over the next few days I prayed and gathered the necessary paperwork. It took about four hours to finalize the entire deal. But I left that Friday, on my birthday, driving a brand new 2015 Honda Odyssey. What a gift! Hallelujah!

One day while driving to the doctor's office, I just started praying intensely. I remembered the minister at bible school saying that we have to pray the word of God back to God. If I ask my heavenly Father in Jesus' name, then it shall be given to me. The more I recited the Scriptures, the more I believed in what I was saying. I declared that I was carrying a baby girl. The doctor told me that I had a less than thirty percent chance of having a daughter. I believed in my heart that I was carrying a little boy until I prayed. During the appointment I had a sonogram. The sonographer knew me by name because my three sons were born at the same practice. It even became a joke between me and the staff at the office. They just knew I was going to have another boy.

Little did they know I had an advantage over them; I had great faith in God. Before the sonographer could even tell me, I saw it with my own eyes. I had conceived a girl. I was ecstatic and felt like screaming at the top of my lungs. I was so over-joyed. It was a miracle!

My next gift is my daughter, Mecca! It was my dream to have a little girl. She is my ray of sunshine who brightens my day and keeps me focused. She is God's promise princess to me. He promised her to me after I received my Kingdom assignment. She confirms everything that the Lord has spoken to me. Mecca means, a *"sign from heaven."* God gave her to me as a gift because I believe in the goodness of the Lord. Some days are more challenging than others. On those days I just look to my children and the Lord for strength. There are times when it appears as though I'm stuck and not moving forward. In those moments I am reminded by a small still voice, "Look at Mecca; you're going to make it," and it makes my heart smile. She was born on July 16, 2015 at Holy Cross Hospital. She has a gentle spirit, and I can see God's anointing on her life. She has a way of looking at us as if she is speaking to us through her eyes, and we can feel her energy. I love her so much more than words can express. I am eternally thankful for her. When she grows up I plan on telling her how God has blessed me with her presence. Each of my children are special to me, and they each have a different function. Praise the Lord for giving them to me.

Chapter 11

All Access

"In the beginning the Word already existed. The Word was with God, and the Word was God" (John 1:1, NLT).

In the beginning before the heavens and earth were created, all three were one. There is only one true God. He is a spirit. God is the Almighty, Omnipotent, Omni-Present, Alpha and Omega. The First and the Last, the Beginning and the End. Jehovah Jireh, Elohim, El- Shaddai just to name a few. *God the Father, the Son Jesus Christ, and the Holy Spirit or some refer to as the Holy Ghost.* I used to believe in only "God" denying the power that flows through all three persons. I am a visual person so I used to struggle with the fact that I could not see God.

Through independent study of Scripture, I have gained intimate knowledge of God and His creation. It is amazing to me how much I learned in one year. Previously, I thought people did not become wise until they were seniors. But true wisdom can only come from revelation by God. If I have a question, I ask God. He always answers always in Scripture.

In the Bible there are two parts: The Old Testament and the New Testament. As a believer it is important that I read the entire Bible. I need to know what happened throughout all of the Scriptures. In the Old Testament, I was subjected to death; in the New Testament I am saved from eternal damnation because of Jesus Christ. Whenever I pray I always end my prayers with, "in Jesus name I pray, Amen." Jesus Christ seals the deal! He bore the punishment that I deserve for living a life of sin. He was bruised for my iniquities and by His stripes I am healed. When Jesus died on the cross, it put an end to all things. There is no more poverty, suffering, despair, hatred, oppression, depression, or captivity; even death lost its sting in the grave. Jesus was crucified on a Friday afternoon and rose from the grave early one Sunday morning. My victory is in the resurrection. God has given all authority to Jesus Christ and to anyone who believes in the Son of Man.

No one can enter into the Kingdom of God except through His Son. Jesus is seated in the heavenly realms at the right hand of God. I have access to God because of the sacrifice Jesus made by laying His life down.

Anything I ask for in the name of Jesus Christ, God has already promised to give it to me. Jesus had a mission, and once it was accomplished He ascended into heaven through the clouds. He will return to earth in the same way. I have His Holy Spirit which dwells on the inside of me. It is my moral compass which leads and directs me through life internally. I used to set reminders in my phone; now I pray *"Holy Spirit, bring it back into my remembrance,"* and I remember every time. My two younger children are always putting things in their mouths that they shouldn't have. Before I attempt to take it out I always pray "Holy Spirit I need them to spit it out of their mouth, in Jesus Name I Pray, Amen."

If I lose something around the house, I ask the Holy Spirit to help me find it. Whenever I listen to that quiet, still voice I never miss. The more I expand my capacity to believe God, the more authority I have as a believer to experience His miracles. I have not earned salvation. It has been given to me through the grace of God. When I believed and accepted Jesus Christ as my personal savior, He knew I was going to make a mess of my life before I was even born.

As a child I was baptized out of ritual, so last year I decided to get baptized as an adult. That was a special day for me. I will cherish it until the day I die. I was born again on that day. My baptism signifies the death of my former self. I was submerged into water. Coming out of the water is significant because it represents the resurrection that my spirit has passed over from death to eternal life. Jesus Christ is the incarnate (means in the flesh) word of God. The Holy Spirit is our helper and the guarantee from God of our inheritance that we will receive from the Lord.

"Then God said, Let us make human beings in our image, to be like us. They will reign over the fish in the sea, the birds in the sky, the livestock, all the wild animals on the earth, and the small animals that scurry along the ground" (Genesis 1:26, NLT). *"The Spirit is God's guarantee that he will give us the inheritance he promised and that he has purchased us to be his own people. He did this so we would praise and glorify him"* (Ephesians 1:14, NLT).

Chapter 12

Elite Baby

"So the next generation might know them-even the children not yet born-and they in turn will teach their own children" (Psalm 78:6, NLT).

I am the youngest of four children. Coincidentally, I have given birth to the most grandchildren. Oftentimes I refer to myself as the baby in the family with the most babies. I have lived with my parents all of my adult life. Briefly, I moved away to attend college in Miami, Florida. After I became pregnant with Skyler, I moved back home to Maryland. Having a newborn child is a lot of responsibility for a teenage mom.

Financially, my mother took care of my son and me. She must have shopped the entire nine months preparing for the arrival of the baby. A new life is an exciting time in the household. When the number of children increased, she continued to support us. Some of my siblings had a difficult time dealing with the time and attention we received. As a result, it has impacted their relationships. One of my brothers told my mother she was doing me a disservice by helping me so much. People prey on naïve mothers so they can take advantage of them. She wanted to protect me from those individuals.

Parenting is a life-long commitment. Women see things differently than men. Nothing in this world can compare to the love mothers have for their children. I would go to war for mine, and I know my mother would do the same for us. You cannot fault someone for loving their children, but there is a difference between supporting and enabling someone. She enabled me to become stagnant and not move forward to becoming a responsible adult. I became financially reliant on her. At one point, I could not buy toilet paper for myself. I did not have anything to contribute to the household expenses. Now, I give according to my earnings because it is the right thing to do. Besides, I love and appreciate my parents, and I do not want to be a further burden for them. Without their devotion to my children and me, I may not have reached my full potential. My parents are my backbone. Whether I am writing, in a workshop, or going to church, they are always willing to fill in the gap.

It is comforting to leave my children with family. I am eternally grateful to my loving parents.

God has given me peace with my living situation. People made me feel guilty about all the help I have received over the years. The Lord spared my father's life many years ago because He knew the purpose my dad would serve later in my life. My dad is the second oldest out of six children. He practically raised his younger brothers and sister. Now, he is helping me raise my children.

It is a privilege to have two generations growing up under one roof. Our family is a demonstration of love and unity working together for a greater purpose. Before, the idea of moving out presented anxieties for many different reasons. I am patiently looking forward to one day purchasing my own home. But for now I feel contentment right where I am living.

I have been strategically placed within the **Hines** generation family tree. Living at home is a humbling experience; it is one which I do not take for granted.

Page intentionally left blank.

Chapter 13

Anxiety

"Do not be anxious about anything, but in every situation, by prayer and petition, with thanksgiving, present your requests to God. And the peace of God, which transcends all understanding, will guard your hearts and your minds in Christ Jesus" (Philippians 4:6-7, NIV).

According to the Merriam-Webster Dictionary:

ANXIETY: Fear or nervousness about what might happen. A feeling of wanting to do something very much.

ALCOHOLISM: A medical condition in which someone frequently drinks too much alcohol and becomes unable to live a normal and healthy life.

PANIC ATTACK: An episode of intense fear or apprehension that is of sudden onset.

FEAR: To be afraid of something or someone; to expect or worry about something bad or unpleasant.

SOCIAL ANXIETY DISORDER: An anxiety disorder that is characterized by persistent and exaggerated fear of social situations...in which embarrassment or a negative judgment by others may occur and that causes significant distress, often resulting in an avoidance of such situations and impairment of normal social or occupational activities.

ANTIDEPRESSANT: Used or tending to relieve or prevent psychic depression.

FAITH: Strong belief or trust in someone or something. Belief in the existence of God; strong religious feelings or beliefs.

"So faith comes from hearing, that is, hearing the Good News about Christ" (Romans 10:17, NLT). "Faith is the confidence that what we hope for will actually happen; it gives us assurance about things we cannot see" (Hebrews 11:1, NLT). "Have faith in God, Jesus answered" (Mark 11:22, NIV).

Reflecting on my childhood, I first experienced anxiety at age thirteen, which is typically the age that social anxiety disorder makes itself known. My mother and I were at a shopping center. A swarm of people filled the area that day as we walked around. There was a jewelry stand in the middle of the mall. The shimmery necklaces and beaded bracelets caught my attention. I wanted to get a closer look at the items, but then I thought about mixing in with the crowd. Social phobia kicked in and I panicked and began to shake uncontrollably. I didn't go over to look at the jewelry. I thought this was an isolated incident, but my life was about to be interrupted.

Years later, I faced uneasiness, alcohol abuse, embarrassment, shame, misunderstanding, and confusion. I asked myself, "Why me?" I have never been a shy person. This behavior simply did not make sense to me. I thoroughly enjoyed meeting and talking to new people, so what was happening? Being faced with an extreme nervous condition was out of character for me. I felt powerless and ashamed. I kept silent for over ten years. According to Understanding the Facts about Social Anxiety Disorder on the Anxiety and Depression Association of America's website, 15 million people suffer from social anxiety disorder, and 36 percent wait at least 10 or more years before seeking help. What made it worse for me, was that I am an African American woman, who fell prey to the stigma in our community regarding mental health. Let us just say speaking to a professional is not one of the things we discuss at the dinner table, or at all. It is rare for our community. That being said, I was afraid to open up to my family and friends because I didn't want them to think that I was going *crazy*. Going to counseling is something most people in my culture are not accustomed to doing, especially taking medication for panic attacks. The anxiety issues did not return until my twenties.

After my first son was born, the nervousness really got out of control. I was on edge all the time, experiencing mood swings and fits of rage. The slightest problem would send me in a downward spiral of worry and depression.

FEAR is the acronym for False, Evidence, Appearing, Real and is used to explain the emotion. Fear is a normal emotion but being in a constant state of fear is not normal. In fact it is a "spirit." *"For God has not given us a spirit of fear and timidity, but of power, love, and self-discipline" (2 Timothy 1:7, NLT).*

I constantly focused on the outcome but never on a strategy for solving a problem. On the surface, no one could see how badly I was suffering because I hid it so well. But on the inside, I was in serious turmoil. I was dying slowly in spirit. My soul was in hell. My daily routine was about to be disrupted. Feeling alone, I began to abuse alcohol. At first, I would only drink in social settings, but that quickly changed as my anxiety increased. I started drinking every day: beer, wine, Tequila, whatever I could drink at the time to calm my nerves.

Drinking and driving became a regular occurrence for me. I had an accident in front of the church and it was not the only one. There were many others as a result of driving drunk; however, I only got caught twice by the authorities. God was protecting me from myself. I used to be terrified of driving long distances because of my phobia. My sister used to tease me about being afraid to drive not knowing that I had serious issues going on. It is hard for people to understand something they have never faced themselves. *"Sometimes people just don't understand what they don't understand."* Then the panic attacks started to occur. I would experience numbness in my fingers, tingling sensations, heart palpitations, increased heart rate, and shaking. It would last for minutes, but it seemed like forever.

Stress triggered my panic attacks, and just the fear of the unknown almost all the time gave me anxiety. When I went out in public, I became fearful of whether or not I was going to have an attack. I didn't want to be caught off guard, so I would wear different baseball caps on my head. My rationale for wearing the hats was that if I started shaking, no one would notice it. Wearing hats became my security blanket. The issue was taking over my life. At this point it was very difficult for me to stay employed because of my stress level. I even quit a great job working at a well-known hospital because of my anxiety.

At the height of my nervousness, I started drinking before work. I had a three-liter box of wine in the basement that no one knew about in my household. Every morning around seven, I would sneak downstairs to the basement and drink several large amounts of wine every day just to take the edge off and start my day. I would drive to work intoxicated and smoke a cigarette in the parking lot. I used mouthwash to mask the alcohol smell and go into work. This lasted a few months before one of my co-workers alerted me to the fact that there were rumors about me in the office. I was shocked and could not believe that others had known.

By this time I was totally consumed with alcohol. It was difficult for me to stay employed. What was I thinking? Of course, everyone could smell the liquor on me. I felt humiliated, and I never returned. The stress was overwhelming. I had a false sense of security whenever I consumed liquor, and I lacked sound judgement. I endangered so many lives driving drunk, including my own. It was irresponsible and selfish not to mention dangerous. Being intoxicated was the only thing that mattered to me. I was hurtful to those who loved me the most. My family endured a lot.

Everything came to a screeching halt when I was arrested for driving while under the influence. This was about three years ago after I left a bar with a former friend. We were both legally drunk and in no condition to be driving. I was behind the wheel that night while speeding down a dark road doing 60mph in a 40 mile zone. The police cruiser was sitting along the side of the road. All of a sudden, I could see flashing lights in my rear view mirror. I pulled over. The officer asked for my license and registration. He proceeded to run my tag number and check to see if my registration was valid. When he came back to my car, he began to question me. He asked me to step out of the car. This is never a good thing, especially if you are under the influence of any substance. The officer asked me to perform a sobriety test. I failed it. He arrested me.

I called my boyfriend at the time to get me from the police station. Needless to say, he was furious and had his own line of questioning. It took over a year to have my day in court. I ended up pleading to a *probation before judgement.* It was not an admission of guilt, but I did acknowledge that there was enough evidence to take me to trial. I was sentenced to a treatment class I now had another class for reckless endangerment, penalty fine, court costs, and lawyer fees. In the end, it cost me thousands of dollars, not to mention embarrassment. I underwent the scrutiny and ridicule by loved ones. I was an alcoholic. I was dealing with many issues in my life during that time*: depression, anger, and fear of the unknown became a way of life for me.* My lifestyle forced me to take a deeper look into my inner spirit. I already knew why I was abusing alcohol. It was because of my anxiety issues, but why did I have anxiety? It was because I had no faith in God and no spiritual foundation in place.

During my recovery period I was diagnosed with *"social anxiety disorder"* and offered medication for treatment. I declined the medicine and opted for counseling instead. Today I am alcohol and anxiety free, and it is only by the grace God. I replaced the fear of the unknown with faith. For I walk by faith and not by sight. I did it! I thank God for calling me out of darkness into the light.

"For we live by faith, not by sight" (2 Corinthians 5:7, NIV).

Chapter 14

Distractions

"I am saying this for your benefit, not to place restrictions on you. I want you to do whatever will help you serve the Lord best, with as few distractions as possible" (1 Corinthians 7:35, NLT).

Distractions can either be good or bad situations to encounter. I have experienced both. It seems like I had more bad distractions during the course of writing my story. Another word for these distractions is opposition. It is the constant battle being waged in the heavenly realms. The enemy used the people who were the closest to me so that I would focus only on my problems and forget about God's promises.

The enemy would constantly use my ex-boyfriend to distract me from going forward. We argued all the time, sometimes to the point where I thought he could possibly become violent. One of those arguments erupted while he was driving my vehicle. The two younger children were with me. We had a verbal dispute, and I insisted that he get out but he refused. Instead, he continued to drive even faster. We were wrestling to keep the car on the road. I tried to call the police so they could find our traveling vehicle, but this only made matters worse. He snatched my cellular phone and threatened to throw it out of the window, knowing that all of my business contacts and content for my book were stored in my phone. It was a plot against me.

During the course of a single week, he called me ninety-nine times in all. This was not by mistake. The enemy kept using him to keep my focus off of being productive. No one should call anyone that many times for any reason. I changed his name in my contact information from his personal name to *"distraction,"* then to *"opposition"* as a reminder to not answer any of his calls.

Another distraction occurred while I was at Bible school. I received a phone call from one of my friends. She told me the baby sitter had dropped my infant. I was frantic and did not know what to do. So I called the baby sitter first to get the details. A lot of emotions ran through my mind. I did not know if I should stay in class or go home to my children. In the moment I felt lost and confused. Eventually I decided to stay. One of the ministers prayed with me after class was over. When I got home, she gave me the full report. She actually rolled off the couch onto the carpet. The fall shocked her more than anything. She was alright with no injuries.

Another example of God's goodness is when I dropped my flash drive with important data on it in water while rushing to get to work one morning. When that happened I did not worry about anything. I prayed. Days later after it had a chance to dry out, it still worked. Bills from previous accounts started coming to me in the mail dating back several years. It seemed like every time I paid a past due bill, here comes another one. Then red light tickets and tickets from other people driving my car came in the mail. Everywhere I turned, there was opposition on all sides. I continued to pray. I cannot forget about the nay-sayers, dream killers, or spiritual assassins. These are people who are always negative. They never see any good in the situation. It seems like they only look for the negative and wait for the person's demise. They can manage to tell me what is impossible to do. But with God all things are possible. I have associates and family members who fall into this category. I love them dearly, but I cannot share my dreams with them. If you are not a dreamer, it is difficult to understand someone who is a dreamer. I pray for those individuals and continue to move forward.

Studying the Word of God helps me to stay focused and in constant prayer. I study instead of worrying about tomorrow because tomorrow has enough worries by itself. Each day offers enough challenges. Meditation is a key component to having a sound mind. I had to re-program my mindset. Everything that I learned prior to accepting Christ as my risen Savior, I threw out. I am a re-educated tree in my family.

Life can also present unexpected distractions. I have lost one family member and a friend of the family. These deaths were unexpected and took me by surprise. I went through a brief grievance process. To be absent from the body is to be present with the Lord. Knowing that gave me peace. I have to take extreme caution whenever a *"good thing"* comes around. Too much of a good thing is not always best for me. I had offers for an all-expenses paid vacation to California, the Bahamas, and Hawaii. But I turned those offers all down because I knew it was a well-orchestrated plot to distract me. Distractions are very subtle. If I'm not careful I can find myself off course. No matter what is going on, to, or around me, I am able to maintain my focus now. I pause, pray, pass, and then push forward into my destiny.

Page intentionally left blank.

Chapter 15

Depression

"For my yoke is easy to bear, and the burden I give you is light" (Matthew 11:30, NLT).

I have been keeping a secret from my family. For two years I have been suffering in silence with post-partum depression. I am breaking my silence because this depression is a silent killer among mothers. Depression is a serious condition that affects the mind. The enemy attacks us in our thought life. I didn't experience it with my first two children. It began after I gave birth to my third child.

Initially I was extremely excited about the birth of my child. But as the weeks went by, I began to feel sad for no apparent reason. Then crazy thoughts started running through my mind. Ungodly thoughts of doing things to my children. It felt like I was going insane. Eventually I told my ex-boyfriend that I was suffering with this issue. But he didn't understand what was happening to me.

Post-partum depression is not a disease; it is a demonic spirit. The adversary was trying to destroy me and my daughter and prevent me from telling my story to help others who are in bondage. There are demonic spirits waiting to enter into our earthly vessels. It is possible that somewhere along the way I came into contact with another individual with that same unholy mindset, with the intentions of destroying an entire family if given the opportunity. I was able to overcome this battle by faith. Others may need to seek counseling or medical attention. If you know someone who you think might be struggling with similar issues, reach out to them in love. The most effective thing you can do is pray for their deliverance.

One of my family members who checked on me regularly asked if I had been struggling with depression. I lied and told her no. After surviving a life-threatening experience, I couldn't fathom struggling with this. It was a scary time. What was going on with me? The adversary was attacking me in bunches. Satan sent in a flood of attacks, but God placed a shield of protection around me.

"From the west, people will fear the name of the LORD, and from the rising of the sun, they will revere

his glory. *For he will come like a pent-up flood that the breath of the LORD drives along" (Isaiah 59:19, NIV).* I felt trapped between good and evil, and I had to win. The depression went from bad to worse after my fourth child, Mecca, was born. None of my previous children were criers. She would constantly cry and scratch her face until it bled. It became unbearable for me at times. I would give her to my mother so I could have a break. During those moments the enemy would whisper horrible things in my ear to do to her. Immediately, I would dismiss those thoughts. She was God's gift to me and a blessing. There was no way on earth that I would ever intentionally hurt any of my children. I began to pray and cry out to the Lord for help. The enemy was trying to use me to destroy my greatest accomplishment, my children. I relied heavily on my faith in God.

Satan cannot do anything to me without God's permission. Even Satan has respect for God's authority. He was created by Him first. God allowed me to go through this experience to give me a voice to speak out on it. *"A final word: Be strong in the Lord and in his mighty power. Put on all of God's armor so that you will be able to stand firm against all strategies of the devil" (Ephesians 6:10-11, NLT).*

Page intentionally left blank.

Chapter 16

Forgiveness

"But if you refuse to forgive others, your Father will not forgive your sins" (Matthew 6:15, NLT).

I asked the Lord for forgiveness with a sincere heart. I had to forgive others, but I had to forgive myself first. It took me awhile to realize that I was mad at me. For many years I harbored resentment towards my mother. It was from a past hurt that occurred when I was a teenager. When you are hurt by someone close to you, it makes it difficult to trust other people. Hurt people end up hurting others. I carried this grudge for thirteen years. I struggled to respect her as a mother.

As a child you look to your parents to be like super heroes. They are there to protect and shield you, not to hurt you emotionally. Having my own children has changed my perspective on parenting. Parents are just people, and they are not perfect. We are all flawed individuals trying to get right with God. When I repented, God forgave me of all of my sins and cast them into the sea of forgetfulness. If God can forgive me, who am I not to forgive others? As I grow spiritually, my confidence in the Lord grows. Reading my Bible really helped me through my darkest hours and increased my faith. It gave me a better understanding of who I am as a child and friend of God. *"For all have sinned and fall short of the glory of God" (Romans 3:23, NIV).*

One day as I sat down with my mom, we had a conversation about the way I treated her over the years. I apologized to her for being a disobedient child. I could feel all of the anger and frustration I was holding on the inside of me being released. I know my parents have done their best to raise my siblings and me with the wisdom they have been given. There is nothing that I hold against them anymore. They have supported me even when my choices in life were contrary to how I was raised.

My parents allowed me to make my own decisions. Most of the time the outcome was not in my favor, but they never stopped loving me. They have always shown me unconditional love. I have always had their support, and I know they love their grandchildren more than life itself. After I apologized to my mother, it was like a weight had been lifted from my chest. Instantly, I felt relieved from carrying around that emotional baggage that was weighing me down spiritually and impacting my relationship with others. You never know how unresolved hurts from the past can affect your present and future relationships. I had to forgive my mother because Christ forgave me first.

When Jesus died on the cross, He suffered for us all. So why was I suffering? After I forgave myself and my mother, it was time for me to forgive everyone else. I struggled for a very long time to forgive my last children's father. God said do not let the sun go down and be angry with anyone. Knowing this, how could I continue to hold a grudge against him? Especially knowing that everything was not all his fault. I was a broken woman who attracted a broken man. God will never call two broken individuals in holy matrimony. Both of the people have to come into the relationship as whole persons. Being whole means having your soul intact. Your soul consists of your desires, mind, and emotions. He was not my enemy. The adversary is the enemy, and he will use those closest to you to try and destroy you. Many times I have allowed the enemy to use me to bring him down. Now that I am aware of it, Satan can no longer use me in that capacity. I am a child of

God, and we should lift up each other instead of tearing down one another. With time, things are getting better now. In the meantime, I continue to pray for his full restoration and complete and total healing. I never meant to hurt him, and I know in my heart that we will be good friends again one day.

My sister and I have been in a turbulent relationship for years. We are eighteen months apart, and my sister has always thought she was my boss. We have feuded mostly in verbal disagreements. But there have been times when we have physically fought. Thank God neither of us was ever seriously injured; we only injured our pride. One time we stopped speaking to each other for almost an entire year, and we lived in the same household. Friends told me to forget about my sister, but I knew in my spirit that that was bad advice. God doesn't make any mistakes, He designated us to be sisters long ago. It was up to us to make the best out of the situation. I made up in my mind that I was not going to fight anymore. She is my sister, and none of us are perfect. I remember when I forgave her I was in my bathroom praying, and I told the Lord that I forgive her for everything that she has ever done to me in the past.

As I began to rejoice and praise the Lord, I had a praise and worship service all by myself. After that moment, I made a conscious decision to work on our relationship. Today our sisterhood is stronger than ever. We can come to each other for advice, and soon I will be the maid of honor in her wedding ceremony. Once we reconciled, I called people that I had offended and apologized to them. We now enjoy harmony and peace in our relationship.

Pocket of Peace Prayer

(With God and His Son)

by Calvin L. Riley – Founder/CED/Coach
Masterpiece Creative Living™ Masterpiece Mentors 360°™

Heavenly Father,
Thank you for making a way for me to have
a relationship with you.

I realize that we all have sinned and need forgiveness; so
here I am and I need forgiveness, and I am hopelessly lost without you. Thank you for being the perfect Father.

I ask you Jesus to be my Savior and my Lord.
I believe that you died for me. I want to turn away from all
my sins. I repent and receive Your Life in exchange for
my sins and my life.

I choose to trust and follow your will, your ways, and your
words. I now invite you to come into my heart and my life.

In Jesus name Amen

This is the first step
Now you need to strengthen unto maturity your faith,
favor and freedom through your relationship with God.

Talk to God every day through Prayer.
Prepare for things that will get worse before
they get better.

Live your life with evidence of concern for other people.
Beware of any "Me, Myself, and I" principles.
Learn how to identity the loveless, compromising, corrupt,
dead, or lukewarm.

Learn how to look good while being persecuted.
Learn how to reach for the hundred-fold life.

The Prayer of Release

by Calvin L. Riley – Founder/CED/Coach
Masterpiece Creative Living™ Masterpiece Mentors 360°™

*Father God; First of all, I just want to say
Thank you*

*I want to thank you for the relationship that I have with you
as an adopted son (daughter) into the Kingdom;*

*I want to thank you for the relationship that I have with my
Blood Brother Jesus who died on the Cross and shed His Blood for
my sins so I might not be held back by my past;*

*I want to thank you for the relationship that I have with the
Holy Spirit; which is the third person of the Godhead and the
Power to disassemble and reassemble the resources of the Father
and the Son;*

*Now I step into my position of authority so I might bind on
Earth as it has been bound in Heaven and loose on Earth as it
has been loosed in Heaven and still you will get all the Honor and
Glory for the rest of my life.*

Now I resubmit myself under your authority so that you
may use me as your Priest, Prophet or King (Queen) this day;
according to your will, your ways and your words.

In Jesus name Amen

MONIQUE V. HINES, AUTHOR

"Together, we walk in faith."

To contact the author for speaking engagements, please refer to her website at www.right-wayliving.com, or by email monique@right-wayliving.com.